CLASSIC
AMERICAN
FARM
TRACTORS

Osprey Colour Series

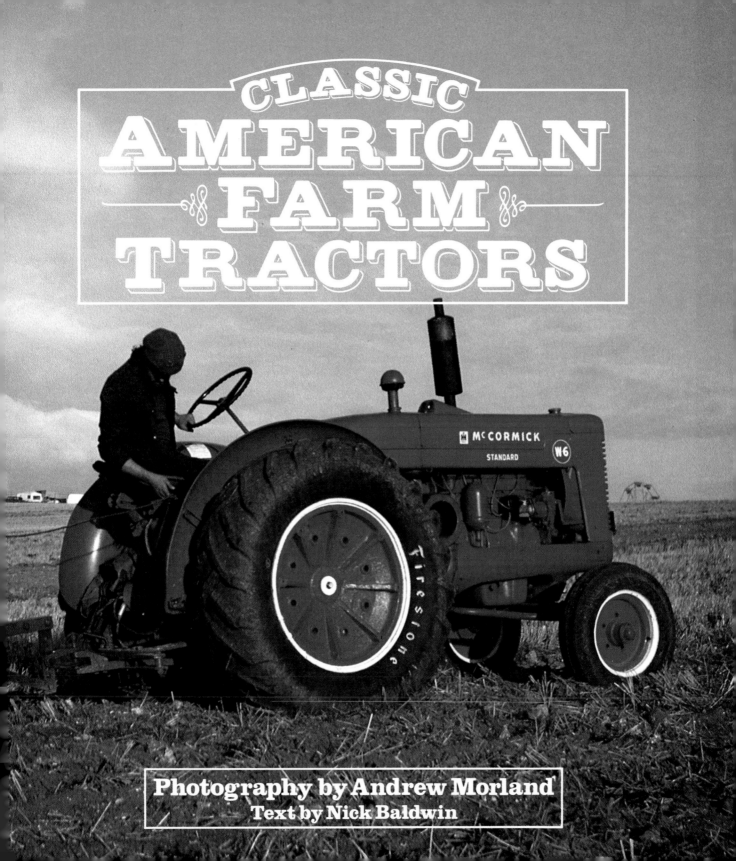

CLASSIC
AMERICAN
FARM
TRACTORS

McCORMICK
STANDARD
W6

Photography by Andrew Morland
Text by Nick Baldwin

Published in 1985 by Osprey Publishing Limited
12–14 Long Acre, London WC2E 9 LP
Member company of the George Philip Group

British Library Cataloguing in Publication Data
Morland, Andrew
    Classic American farm tractors.—(Osprey colour series)
    1. Farm tractors—United States
    I. Title
    629.2′25   TL233
ISBN 0-85045-617-7

Editor Tim Parker
Printed in Italy

Contents

Introduction

Why *Classic American Farm Tractors*? If you have flipped through the pages already, you'll know why. If you haven't, then there's only one quick answer.

A longer answer is that there is around the world a strong enthusiasm for old machinery of all kinds. Now that we are well into computer and space technology, and in some cases even ordinary folk are beginning to understand how such things work, we have an inherent yearning to look back and study the simple things. If they can been seen to work before our very eyes, so much the better. If that old machinery is colourful and somehow 'oddball', things get better still. Add a third ingredient, American content, and everyone is happy. Lest we forget, the non-American English speaker somehow looks to America, at least, for agricultural machinery and the native American knows what's best is homegrown. We, thus, have put together 120 all colour photographs of American sourced tractors which we have chosen to call 'classic' as a euphemism for 'old'. Many of the shots show the tractors working, or should we say operating. Most were shot either in England or Canada.

For this title in the Osprey Colour Series, which concentrates broadly on transport, we have used two experts – the photographs were taken by Andrew Morland and the captions were written by Nick Baldwin. Both are renowned in their own fields – Andrew has long been shooting all forms of transport around the world and having it published also in many forms. This is his fifth book in this series.

Nick Baldwin is something of a truck and tractor expert. He has written a number of books and regularly contributes to magazines. Like Andrew he runs and restores his own historic vehicles. Nevertheless putting such a book together takes more than photographer, writer and publisher. In this particular case, it's taken dozens of people. For a start there are all the tractor owners, event organizers and honest enthusiasts who have gone out of their way to help. Most of them remain anonymous but that doesn't in any way dilute our gratitude to them. They are no less important than those people and organizations which are named.

A great deal of photography took place at two museums. In order of volume we have to thank the Ontario Agricultural Museum at Milton in Canada first. This superb outdoor complex was conceived in 1966 by the Ontario Government essentially around a collection of equipment assembled by a Mr Charles Matthews of Langstaff, Ontario. It was opened in 1979 and has flourished ever since under the Ontario Ministry of Agriculture and Food. Look at the photographs which are credited *OAM* to see just how good it is. Mr Albert Fife was the man on the ground there – if ever there is a man to start old tractors, it's Mr Fife.

The second museum is the Hunday Museum, otherwise known as The National Tractor and Farm Museum at West Side, Newton, Stocksfield-on-Tyne in the north of England. This was started by John Moffitt who collected old tractors from around the world and named his museum after his famous Hunday Friesian herd. Again, it's a superb place, a model museum carefully run by curator Mr Less Blackmore. All photographs shot at the Hunday Museum are captioned *NTFM*.

Special thanks must go to The South Somerset Agricultural Preservation Club (Hon. Sec., Shenley, West Bagborough, nr Taunton, Somerset). This club organizes 'Yesterday's Farming' at the Bath and West Showground near Shepton Mallet amongst other meetings.

More thanks must go to The Great Dorset Steam Fair Limited (Show Secretary, Show Office, Dairy Mead, Child Okeford, Blandford Forum, Dorset) who organize the Stourpaine Bushes 'Great Working of Steam Engines' annually in September.

Finally thanks must go to the Yeovil Festival of Transport (Yeovil Car Club Secretary, 30 The Crescent, Yeovil, Somerset) whose August annual meeting hosts likeminded tractor enthusiasts. Without all these people there would have been no photographs and book. Thank you all.

1 Allis-Chalmers and OilPull Rumely

Allis-Chalmers

LEFT Allis-Chalmers had joined the United Tractor and Equipment Corporation in 1929 to produce the United tractor as part of a wide range of co-operative farm machinery. The Corporation soon failed but from its ashes came the famous Allis U. Here's Mr M. Fleet's 1942 model

BELOW The United Tractor had used proprietary Continental engines but for 1933 and onwards Allis-Chalmers made their own 34 hp overhead valve four-cylinder UM engine for the Model U

BELOW Allis-Chalmers got into the crawler business in 1928 with the acquisition of the Monarch Tractor Corporation. From the Monarch evolved the Model M in the 1930s using many components in common with the Model U. This is a 1941 model WM

RIGHT The Model WM could handle a three to four furrow plough in heavy ground. Photographed at Stourpaine Bushes, owner Draper of Salisbury

BELOW RIGHT The Allis-Chalmers Model B was built for 20 years from 1937, during which time over 125,000 were sold. It was one of the best all-round tractors in the 20 hp class for many years. This is a 1945 model belonging to Mr D. Dear, shot at Yeovil Festival of Transport

A 1942 Model B with the original 13/16 hp four-cylinder engine that was enlarged in 1944. Despite the relatively light-weight appearance this Model B packed 1500 lb drawbar pull

BELOW The little orange Allis tractors have survived very well despite their apparently skimpy construction. This 1951 Model B has a young driver under careful supervision

RIGHT There can hardly be a tractor rally nowadays that does not feature at any rate one small Allis-Chalmers Model B. From 1937 to 1950 nearly 115,000 were sold

15

OilPull Rumely

LEFT The unconventional looking Rumely OilPull was built in a variety of sizes at La Porte, Indiana from 1909 up to the company's takeover by Allis-Chalmers in 1931. (*Ontario Agricultural Museum, Milton, Canada; or OAM*)

BELOW Part of the success of the OilPull was its radiator stack containing oil that was cooled by the induced draft from the engine exhaust. (*OAM*)

LEFT Like so many of their contemporaries Rumely tractors had transverse engines and direct gear drive to the rear wheels. Their OilPulls of 12 to 40 drawbar were remarkably popular, some 56,500 being produced in all. (*OAM*)

BELOW Low grades of kerosene could be burned by OilPulls thanks to special Secor-Higgins carburettors and the scientifically matched relatively hot running of the engine. This was the work of John Secor with the Rumely family, who were of German extraction and knew Dr Diesel. Albert Fife drives. (*OAM*)

The Rumely business grew from a small blacksmithy opened at La Porte in 1852. It went on to make steam engines and threshers before adopting internal combustion for its tractors in 1909. (*OAM*)

RIGHT Rumely tried to create a miniature International Harvester set up by acquiring firms that gave it a fuller line of equipment to offer. It bought the Gaar, Scott traction engine firm, the Aultman and Taylor tractor business, Advance Threshers and others but lost much money in Russia and Canada. (*OAM*)

BELOW A classic late model Oilpull showing that some attempt had been made to give it 'styling' rather than a strictly functional appearance. This look was retained into 1930, but by then there were few customers for such apparently archaic designs and Allis-Chalmers had to come to the rescue. (*OAM*)

2 Case plus Emerson-Brantingham, Rock Island and Wallis

Case

A fine Cross-Motor Case in the sort of original and unmodified state that every vintage tractor collector dreams of finding such a desirable model. Even traces of the original grey and red paintwork remain. (*The National Tractor and Farm Museum, Newton, Stocksfield-on-Tyne, England; or NTFM*)

A restored Cross-Motor Case, so called because of the transverse engine. Unlike so many of its rivals the cylinders were upright and stayed in this position from 1916 to 1930. (*OAM*)

The 12/20 hp model of Cross-Motor Case, current from
1922 to 1928, had these ingenious pressed steel wheels,
as did its short-lived Model A successor of 1928 to 1930.
The position of the four-cylinder engine simplified the
transmission and gave excellent weight distribution.
(*OAM*)

RIGHT The famous Old Abe emblem adopted by Jerome Increase Case for his threshing machine business in 1865 and later used on the tractors. The Bald Eagle had served as a regimental mascot in the American Civil War and was named after President Abraham Lincoln. (*OAM*)

BELOW This view gives an excellent impression of the compact dimensions of the smallest Cross-Motor. Larger models had channel-steel chassis in place of castings. (*OAM*)

ABOVE Detail view of air-cleaner side and valve cover of typical late Cross-Motor Case. (*OAM*)

LEFT With all its serious rivals since the first Fordson adopting a longitudinal engine position, Case was forced to bow to the inevitable. Following its takeover of Emerson-Brantingham in 1928 it introduced a conventional tractor in the following year, the Model L. Then in 1930 came its smaller brother, the 17/27 hp Model C of which a 1939 example is shown here. Shot at Stourpaine

ABOVE The DEX was one of a family of 'three plough capacity' 26/32 hp models. They were sent to Britain to boost food production during the Second World War and performed admirably

LEFT In the late 1930's angular tractors started to go out of fashion and most of the big firms adopted some form of 'streamlining'. At Case this involved a bulbous grille, a radiator cap with swept wings and a new house colour of Flambeau Red. Here we see a 1941 DEX incorporating these features. Owned by the Osborne brothers

ABOVE A wartime Case poised for work with an implement that has yet to be restored. This outfit is in Britain, where Case earned an enviable reputation but was then little heard of until its takeover of the David Brown tractor business. (*NTFM*)

LEFT The Case LA was a modernized version of the former L model with four gears instead of three. It had a 32/45 hp ohv engine and was a well-liked machine, especially amongst contractors who needed high power at the belt pulley. Introduced in 1940, this is a 1948 example

ABOVE When most Case models went for full 'styling' the little 18 hp 'one plow' RC model, adopted a more restrained 'sunburst' radiator grille. Here we see a 1939 example owned by the Osborne brothers

Emerson-Brantingham

Emerson-Brantinghams, made in Rockford, Illinois, were distinctive-looking tractors in the 'teens and 1920s. With their large wheels driven by internal ring gearing, their low bonnet line and high driving position behind a transverse fuel tank, they could not be mistaken for anything else. In 1928 Case bought the firm to gain access to its designs. (*NTFM*)

Rock Island

The Rock Island Plow Co. made implements and added tractors in 1916 when it took over the Heider line. These continued under the Heider name for many years but in the later 1920s the Rock Island title was gradually adopted. In 1937 Case acquired the company and discontinued the tractors. (*NTFM*)

Wallis

The J.I. Case Plow works made Wallis tractors and pioneered unit-frame construction in 1912/13. They were independent of the Case threshing machine business and in 1928 were acquired by Massey-Harris. Meanwhile, Ruston and Hornsby had been building the Wallis under licence in Britain. Here we have a 1930 Massey-type Wallis 20/30 still featuring the curved plate unit construction. (*OAM*)

3 John Deere and Waterloo Boy

John Deere

In 1912 the famous John Deere plough business decided to enter the tractor field and after various false starts its famous twin-cylinder Model D became its first really successful model in 1924 and was produced for some 30 years. A close-up shows an early example with ingenious pressed-steel cleats and rubber road band. All are on loan from the John Deere corporation. (*OAM*)

The John Deere Model B was a small tractor (initially 9/14 hp when introduced in 1935) that was to remain in the range until 1952. This is a 1939 example

The Model B featured the familiar twin-cylinder layout with the engine lying horizontally with its head just behind the radiator. The Model B came in various layouts indicated by a second serial letter. This is a BR indicating low, standard build, fixed axle shot at Ham Hill in Somerset, England

From 1938, in line with other American manufacturers, attempts to make a more modern and stylish product, meant that John Deere gradually adopted the styling shown here. Their tricycle models were available with single or twin close-set front wheels; here at Stoneleigh in Warwickshire, England

A 1939 tricycle version of a Model H preserved in
Somerset by Mr J. Chard of Axbridge. The H was a 12
hp machine current between 1939 and 1947 and usually
used as a row-crop tractor

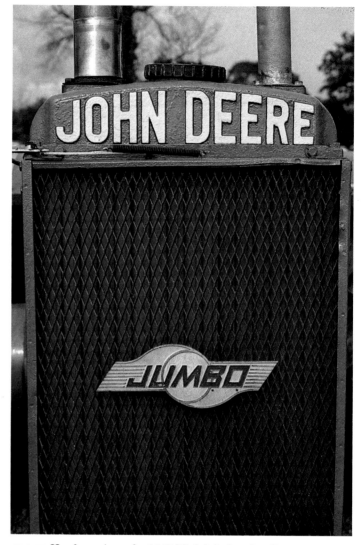

ABOVE Head on view of a 1940 Model A showing the radiator protective mesh that also contained a blind. The Jumbo nickname is a later addition, though quite appropriate as the A was said to be able to replace a six horse team (or one elephant!)

LEFT An attractively restored John Deere posed at a West Country agricultural machinery rally, actually the Yeovil Festival of Transport. Note the neat winch installation and the usual 'flat' engine layout

Waterloo Boy

John Deere's first successful tractor was acquired when they took over the Waterloo Gasoline Engine Co. in 1918 for $2.1 million. Nearly 20,000 of these Model N 12/125 hp Waterloo Boys were made until 1924 and this one dates from 1918 and is owned by Mr M. Ockwell of Swindon

LEFT The first pattern of Fordson entered series production in 1917 and could be identified by the ladder-sided radiator. Nearly all the early ones were sent to Britain to boost agricultural output. This one is on view at Bicton Gardens in Devon

BELOW The Fordson was the first cast iron frame, unit-construction tractor. This ensured strength, perfect alignment for prolonged engine/transmission life and ultimately such a low cost that Ford was able to capture 75 per cent of the American market in the early 1920s. (*Bicton Gardens*)

4 Fordson versus Samson (aka General Motors)

Fordson

A British-built Fordson developed for airfield use in the Second World War. It had Roadless tracks and a Hesford front-mounted winch. Fordsons were modified for all manner of agricultural and industrial purposes

The green livery came to the Standard Fordson Model N in 1940, partly because the previous orange paintwork had made them too visible in wartime service. These are views of a nicely restored 1942 example

ABOVE A Model N ploughing during a South Somerset Agricultural Preservation Club meeting. The N was the backbone of mechanised farming in many countries during its long production life between 1929 and 1945 and, of course, went on earning its keep on many small farms until comparatively recent times

RIGHT A rather unusual colour scheme on a preserved Fordson N. This one dates from 1943 and has the usual 27 hp four-cylinder petrol/TVO engine that gave such sterling service over the years

Samson

The Samson Sieve-Grip tractor made in Stockton, California enjoyed some success, due in part to the low ground pressure imparted by its broad wheels with open treads. When it became obvious that Ford was going to make tractors their arch rivals General Motors' president W. C. Durant looked around for a suitable counter design. In February 1917 he acquired Samson

General Motors soon designed a more conventional tractor, the Model M, to compete with Ford but general postwar difficulties in the motor business led their new president Pierre S. Du Pont to shut down the unprofitable parts. The Samson Tractor Division became an early victim in 1922

5 International Harvester including Farmall, McCormick-Deering, Mogul and Titan

International

LEFT International's McCormick-Deering division came up with a 15/30 tractor in 1921 incorporating all the best and latest features and added the 10/20 type shown here two years later. This is a 1927 example. Owned by Mr Fowler

BELOW The International Junior 8/16 hp was current between 1917 and 1922. It was more advanced than other Internationals at that time, but still featured such primitive features as a separate channel frame and chain drive. The radiator behind the engine kept it away from dust and damage. The engine itself was an advanced ohv four-cylinder unit. Owned by Mr M. Ockwell

International engineers worked from the time of the
First World War to make a truly universal tractor. It
would be able to have front, rear or mid-mounted
implements and easily convertible row-crop features.
The first few Farmalls, as they were called, were made
in 1923. These were slowly accepted and the first year's
22 tractors became 4430 in 1926 and 9502 in 1927.
(*NTFM*)

Farmall

The Farmall F-12 from International's McCormick-Deering division was the smallest of the series and was made from 1932 to 1938. Total Farmall production by the latter date was an impressive 420,460. Note the 'over the top' steering gear arrangements that made tricycle or standard front axle readily interchangeable. Farmalls were grey with red wheels to late 1936, when they became red all over. (*OAM*)

The little Farmall Model A introduced in 1939 developed 16.32 drawbar horsepower and 18.34 belt horsepower in its Nebraska test. Like other Farmalls it had step-down gearing at the ends of the rear axle for maximum crop clearance. This is Mr D. Lock's 1940 example at a SSAD Club meeting

Amongst many clever features of the Farmall A was its so-called Culti-Vision. This referred to the engine offset to nearside seat to the offside that gave the operator an unhindered forward view, very helpful when working in row-crops. (*Yeovil*)

RIGHT The Farmall M appeared in America in 1939 and became popular in Britain. From 1949 examples were produced at Doncaster as the BM and then in 1952 came a diesel version, the BMD. Here a BMD tows a No. 42 International combine harvester, of which nearly 25,000 were made during the Second World War. (*Stoneleigh*)

BELOW The distinctive appearance of a McCormick W6 in close-up.This model spanned the war years and ended in 1953. It developed 33 drawbar horsepower, making it suitable for three furrow ploughs. There was also a diesel version known as the WD6

RIGHT An attractive combination; driver Pearl Friend. The tractor is a 1958 Farmall Super BMD, which was a British built version of the M diesel offered from 1953. It offered big power (43/48 hp) and was a very popular machine on larger farms. (*Yeovil*)

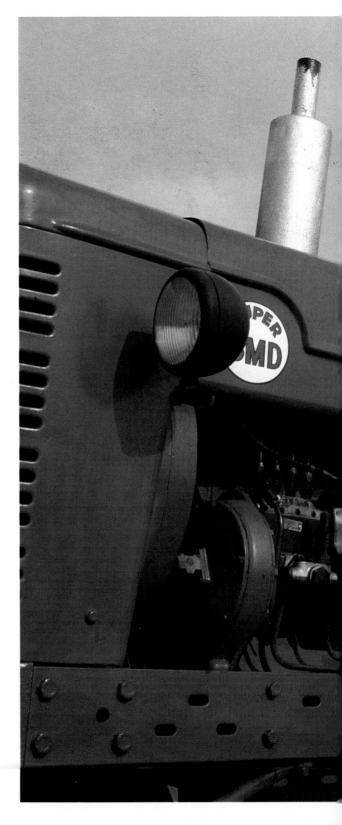

BELOW The old Farmall F series was phased out in 1939 and in its place came such models as the A, B, H and M. Shown here is a 1944 H with the familiar feature of a quickly adjustable rear wheel track. On Nebraska test the H developed 24.2 drawbar horsepower

LEFT The belt pulley side of a 1959 Farmall BMD where 36 hp was developed as compared with 31 hp at the drawbar. In all some 300,000 of the M series were produced

ABOVE A 1950 Farmall BMD that has survived into the preservation era, though a few others are still in regular work. International's British operations based at Doncaster were expanded in the 1950s to include the former Jowett car and van factory at Idle, Bradford

McCormick-Deering

Two of the cornerstones of the International Harvester
Company formed in 1902 were the implement factories
created by Cyrus Hall McCormick and William Deering
in the previous century. Their names were retained on
the tractors for many years, and that of McCormick
even after the Second World War. (*OAM*)

A beautifully restored McCormick-Deering W-40. This was a relatively rare high power six-cylinder model current between 1934 and 1940. Roughly 6500 were made plus 3400 of the WD-40, which was America's first standard production diesel tractor. (*OAM*)

Two views of a 1932 McCormick-Deering 10/20 breaking up stubble. Sometimes badged simply as an International, the 10/20 was one of the best and most famous tractors ever produced. Naturally it could not hope to compete with contemporary Fordsons on price but its technical specification was far superior. Over 200,000 were sold in its 1923 to 1939 production life whereas in the early 1920s 100,000 Fordsons per year were built. Owner Kingsley Cunningham of Rustington sits aboard

Mogul

Many of the early International tractors were sold
under the Mogul name and included some colossal
traction engine-like machines and the relatively
compact 8/16 shown here that was available in 1914/17.
It had a single-cylinder horizontal engine running on
petrol or paraffin and approximately 14,000 were built.
(*NTFM*)

Titan

Another famous name used on early International tractors was that of Titan. Like the Mogul, it borrowed much from barn engine practice to make it simple to maintain on the farm. It came in a variety of shapes and sizes, but here we have the most common, a 1919 two-cylinder Titan 10-20, of which over 78,000 were sold between 1915 and 1922. (*Stourpaine*)

6 Massey-Harris + Sawyer-Massey = tenuous connection

Massey-Harris

As major farm implement manufacturers Massey-Harris of Toronto, Canada were surprisingly late into the tractor manufacturing business. However, they sold other people's tractors under their own name from 1917. Initially these were by Bull, and then in 1918 by the Parrett Tractor Co. of Chicago, whose machine with unusual radiator position is depicted. (*OAM*)

With the acquisition of the Wallis line from J. I. Case Plow Works in 1928 Massey-Harris became serious tractor manufacturers and in the 1930s offered quite an extensive range. Here we have a tricycle version 'as found' and dragged out of a farm sale for hopeful preservation and restoration. (*NTFM*)

A late 1930s Massey-Harris 101. This was a 35 hp machine featuring Twin-Power, a clever marketing gimmick which was no more complex than alternative governor settings. At the time Massey-Harris were buying their engines from Chrysler and Continental. (*OAM*)

RIGHT The Pacemaker was typical of the 'styled' tractors available at the outbreak of the Second World War. There was also a very similar Challenger model intended primarily for row-crop work

Below A preserved 1942 25 hp example of a Massey-Harris 102 Twin-Power Junior next to a Roadless half-track Fordson Major at a typical summer rally

BELOW An interesting museum exhibit in the shape of a 1949 Massey-Harris 55. The number indicated its horsepower, which actually proved to be 59 on Nebraska test. Both petrol and diesel versions of this model were produced. (*OAM*)

RIGHT Nearly 100,000 of the 44 family of Massey-Harris were built from 1947 to 1955 using both four and six cylinder engines. This is a 1947 744 owned by Mr B. Woodvine. In 1953 Massey-Harris and Ferguson merged to create a massive multi-national 'full-line' competitor to International Harvester. (*Stourpaine*)

Sawyer-Harris

The Sawyer-Massey Co. of Hamilton, Ontario was an important machinery and steam engine builder. Some of its financial backing came from the Massey family, though there was no direct tie-up with Massey-Harris. From steam traction engines it was but a relatively short step to giant internal combustion engined prairie tractors in 1910. The firm never made a successful transition to the smaller tractors that were needed after the Great War, and thereafter concentrated on road making machinery instead. (*OAM*)

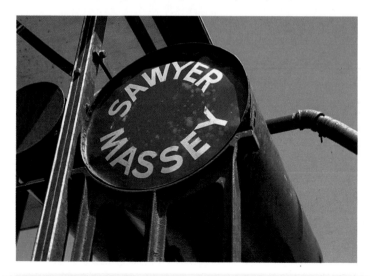

SAWYER
MASSEY
CO. LIMITED
HAMILTON
CANADA

G564

The Sawyer-Masseys used large four-cylinder engines,
mounted in line and vertically above the rear wheels
for optimum traction. Drive was by internal ring gears
in the traction engine type wheels.
Sawyer-Massey made much play in their publicity of
their special knowledge of Canadian farming
requirements. After the Massey family withdrew
financial support in protest at Sawyer's move into 'gas
tractors' there was no way that the Sawyer-Masseys
could compete with the other North American tractor
giants, let alone Massey-Harris. (*OAM*)

7 White Motor Corporation means Cletrac, Cockshutt, Hart-Parr, Minneapolis-Moline, Oliver and Twin City

Cletrac

The Cleveland Motor Plow Co. which became the Cleveland Tractor Co. built crawlers from 1916 and this is a very early example sold under an ingenious slogan. Its Weidley four-cylinder engine 12 drawbar and 20 belt horsepower. All the Cletracs are owned by Charles Doble of Wellington, Somerset

The original Cleveland eventually developed into the K-20 Cletrac. The company's guiding light was Rollin White, who had left the family commercial vehicle firm, where he had been responsible for the design of their early steam cars. He established a ten acre factory in Cleveland to make cars and tractors. The former Rollins were not a success, but the Cletracs most certainly were. (*Doble*)

LEFT The old and the 'new', or to be more precise a mid-1930s Model 80. This one is shown in Britain, where sales were originally handled by truck maker W. G. Burford and then by the well-known Blaw-Knox construction machinery firm. (*Doble*)

BELOW The engine of a Cletrac 80. This is a petrol version with three blocks of two cylinders. Cletrac were one of the pioneers of diesel engined crawlers in 1933 and many 80s subsequently used rather less thirsty diesels. In 1944 the Cletrac business was acquired by Oliver and continued until five years after the White takeover of Oliver in 1960. (*Doble*)

89

Cockshutt

In 1929 Oliver and Hart-Parr merged. One of the first
results was that the Hart-Parr 18-36 was redesigned
with four vertical cylinders as the 18-28. It was sold in
Canada by the Cockshutt Plow Co. of Brantford,
Ontario under their own name. (*OAM*)

Cockshutt's history went back to 1839 and they later became famous for ploughs and harvest machinery. Their tractors were variations on an Oliver theme, in this case of the 1940 to 1948 Row Crop 60. Following the White takeover of Oliver in 1960, the Cockshutt name gradually disappeared from tractors. (*OAM*)

Hart-Parr

LEFT Charles W. Hart and Charles H. Parr were amongst America's most important tractor pioneers. They built their first in 1901 and subsequent models from Charles City, Iowa were typical of the 'barn engine on wheels' concept. Then in 1918 came the New Hart-Parr – a more advanced tractor that survived to the end of the marque's separate existence but still featured horizontal engines. (*OAM*)

BELOW LEFT A view over the magento and twin-cylinders of a Hart-Parr 12-24. As can be seen the engine lay horizontally with most of its weight over the driving wheels. (*OAM*)

BELOW The Hart-Parr 12-24E was made between 1924 and 1928 when it was superceded by the 12-24H, which had a slightly larger cylinder bore. It was described as a 'two-to-three plow' tractor. (*OAM*)

LEFT The Hart-Parr emblem in close-up. Though the firm was not the first to make tractors in America, it was probably the first to have them in series production in 1903. (*OAM*)

RIGHT The driver's view of a typical Hart-Parr of the 1920s. A modern operator would find the two forward and one reverse gears rather inadequate and not helped by the fact that the engine was limited to about 800 rpm. (*OAM*)

BELOW The Hart-Parr 28-50 produced from 1927 to the end of the horizontal engine range's life in 1930 consisted of two 12-24 engines placed side by side and marginally uprated. Two forward gears gave top speeds of 2.26 and 3.2 mph and total weight of the colossus was 8600 lb. (*OAM*)

A 1926 Hart-Parr 18-36 at a West Country rally makes a very rare machine to British eyes. It also makes a pleasant slow thumping sound as it circulates. (*Yeovil*)

Odd man out in a line-up of Allis-Chalmers. Following
the merger with Oliver, Nichols and Shepard and the
American Seeding Machine Co. in 1929, and the
formation of the Oliver Farm Equipment Co., the Hart-
Parr name joined that of Oliver (and Cockshutt) on
tractors for many years. (*Yeovil*)

Minneapolis-Moline

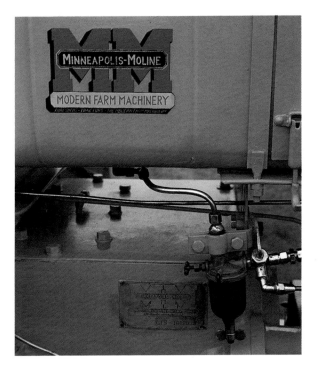

LEFT A 1942 Minneapolis-Moline GTS from a firm that in 1938 called itself the Modern Tractor Pioneers. This was justified by their advanced pressed-steel cab in 1938 and by their high compression tractors from 1935 able to run on leaded fuel. Soon 80 per cent of sales featured high compression engines

RIGHT The MM badge in close-up. Some Minneapolis-Moline models were assembled in France by the Mathis car firm and the MM was shown to stand for Mathis-Moline. Owned by Mr F. Parker of Montacute, Somerset

BELOW The GTS magneto in close-up. An interesting feature of Minneapolis-Molines was the horizontal disposition of the valves that allowed these to be worked by rockers pivotting on the side of the cylinder block. (*Parker*)

1942 GTS from the Minneapolis-Moline Power Implement Co., a firm created in 1929 when the makers of Minneapolis, Twin City and Moline Tractors merged together to create another great American machinery group. Its initial assets were a colossal $24 million. (*Parker*)

The Minneapolis-Moline Model UTS was one of several to arrive in Britain to help food production in the Second World War. The U and Z series were unusual in having five forward gears. The styling on this model was called Visionlined and it had a 40 hp engine suitable for '3 to 4 plows'. Its makers ultimately joined Oliver in the White group in the 1960s. (*OAM*)

Oliver

The Oliver 90 was another of the really great American tractors. It appeared in 1937 and lasted to 1953, when a technically similar 99 replaced it and was produced to 1957. The original 90 was a four-cylinder ohv 443 cu. in. gas, kerosene or distillate engined machine able to replace a 16 mule team and pull a four furrow plough. There was an adjustable governor, electric self-starter, nickel steel cylinder liners and many other advanced features, but not the streamlined styling adopted by so many of its contemporaries. Owned by Mr G. Ball

A classic view of a classic tractor. The Oliver name had
come from Scotsman James Oliver, who had established
a plough factory in Indiana in 1868. The merger of his
Oliver Chilled Plow Company with Hart-Parr and
others in 1929 had created an industrial giant with an
extensive range of high-quality implements

RIGHT Oliver carried their type numbers and purpose on the rear of their bonnet sides. The 60 was a 16.5 horsepower machine produced from 1940 with streamlined styling and a tricycle wheel arrangement on the Row Crop model. (*NTFM*)

BELOW The Oliver 80 was a three-plough tractor with four forward gears allowing up to 5.6 mph at 1200 rpm. Like the 90 it had an advanced ohv engine and was a high-quality tractor with a long working life. From 1940 a diesel version was also offered. Owned by Mr F. Heal

Twin City

The Twin City was a product of Minneapolis Steel and Machinery Co. which merged with the Minneapolis Threshing Machine Co. and the Moline Plow Co, in 1929 to create the Minneapolis-Moline Power Implement Co. The 12/20 model shown was available from 1919 to 1927. (*NTFM*)

RIGHT The tractor's name was derived from the familiar name Twin City for the adjoining Minneapolis and St Paul on the banks of the Mississippi. (*NTFM*)

BELOW A remarkable feature of the Twin City 12/20 was the two overhead inlet and two overhead exhaust valves on each of its four cylinders driven by twin camshafts. This was claimed to improve combustion and therefore power and economy. (*NTFM*)

With the formation of Minneapolis-Moline in 1929 some of the mid-weight Twin City models continued for a time until replaced by new designs in the 1930s. Here we see one of the transitional types with the style of radiator header tank adopted to show the two names. One of the last of the true Twin City models was the 21-32 which continued to 1938, latterly under the name Minneapolis-Moline FTA. (*NTFM*)

8 And some of the rest: Allwork, Co-op, Eagle and Happy Farmer

Allwork

The Electric Wheel Co. of Quincy, Illinois was so named because it was one of the pioneers of metal wheels in the 19th Century. The new-fangled electricity helped its industrial process and was incorporated in the company title. Tractors were made from about 1908 to 1930, this one with transverse four-cylinder engine dating from 1928. The name White on the radiator header tank is nothing to do with the White firm we encountered with Oliver but is Geo. White and Sons who distributed Allwork tractors in Canada. (*OAM*)

Co-op

There have been numerous co-operative attempts to make cheap basic tractors either as part of a farmers' or industrial co-operative. Tractors are made under similar arrangements in both Italy and France but all such attempts in America have met with failure. This Co-op was the work of the Duplex Machinery Co. of Battle Creek, Michigan and lasted briefly in the late 1930s using Chrysler engines. (*OAM*)

Eagle

A very rare Eagle in captivity in England. The Eagle
Manufacturing Co. (not to be confused with Eagle
Engineering of Warwick, England who made the Boon
Colonial tractor) were based at Appleton, Wisconsin
and were one of the pioneer American manufacturers.
Traditional type two-cylinder machines were made for
some 30 years but were joined by more conventional
tractor albeit with six cylinders around 1930

An Eagle in Canada drags out a locally produced
Lobsinger harvester. This is one of the two-cylinder
models with Eagle's own engines whereas the final six-
cylinder types used proprietary motors by Wisconsin
and Hercules. Albert Fife drives in this photograph and
in the next two. (*OAM*)

LEFT Standing is the only way to get a clear view in tight manoeuvres. An idea of the slow engine revolutions when idling is given by the camera's ability to almost 'freeze' the flywheel. This Eagle is a Model H dating from 1927. (*OAM*)

BELOW And so to bed. . . . Sadly for Eagle, who managed to survive alongside their bigger rivals right up to World War 2, it proved to be impossible to get back into tractor production in the 1940s. (*OAM*)

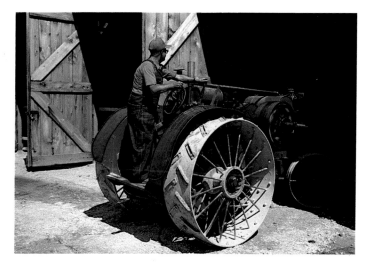

Happy Farmer

The Happy Farm Tractor Co. was a shortlived venture formed in 1915, based in Minneapolis that made a rival to the Waterloo Boy (forerunner of the John Deere tractor) for the La Crosse implement firm to market in preference to Waterloo's tractors. Happy Farmer was soon reorganized along with the Sta-Rite Engine Co., who had actually built many tractors, as the La Crosse Tractor Co. but it fizzled out in the early 1920s. (*OAM*)

The Happy Farmer was a simple and basic machine with a twin-cylinder engine and the exposed valve gear shown here. Also visible is the mechanical oiler, one of the spark plugs and part of the large flywheel needed to keep it running smoothly. (*OAM*)